For —

with to
and friendship and
cheer in a family
reunion that included
list and

Arthur

May 14ᵗʰ 20 5

From Sunshine Road

Poems

Arthur Boardman

VANTAGE PRESS
New York

Cover design by Ximena Cajias

FIRST EDITION

Published by Vantage Press, Inc.
419 Park Ave. South, New York, NY 10016

Manufactured in the United States of America
ISBN: 0-533-15048-5

Library of Congress Catalog Card No.: 2004097245

0 9 8 7 6 5 4 3 2 1

For Pat

Contents

From Sunshine Road

Old Members by the Mimbres

Smiling, we name them to ourselves with play
On "Mimbres," Spanish for the stream that now
Reveals its flow by rocks it carried down
From mountains farther north—dry rocks the white
Of bones, like theirs that mutely speak to us
As pots do they left on skulls often times.

Such treatment of their dead throughout their times
Attests to care, preserved a pot the play
Of thought and hands had formed, and teases us
To guess the thought. Yet there's no way we now
Could know that they conceived there lived in white
Of bones to come a horror to keep down,

Or hoped a graceful crane in gliding down
Within the pot reminded souls of times
When quick brown hands were drawing, black on white,
The strolling bear, or quail, or hares at play,
Making them live and thus the then a now.
Why not? The figures make them live for us.

Some of the pots we have have come to us
Because the picks and shovels digging down
For fenceposts or rails or gold happened now
And then upon some artifacts from times
Long gone—profit unlooked for in the play
Of yucca brushes brushing black on white.

Such spoils stand in the artificial white
Of neon lights today, displayed for us
To try to puzzle out the meanings play
Of minds and will and supple hands set down
On little concave walls of clay in times
Of stars less dimmed by light than those of now,

Or we smile as a smiling speaker now
Points to the way a shape in black on white
Suavely becomes a white on black at times,
Or as a living artist, just for us,
Looks in the pots with care and copies down
The beasts and birds that always seem at play.

Old members now can't guess the smiles from us
Are meant for them. The white they lined brings down,
Even in times of rain, the sun of play.

Columbus NM 88029

Among these houses set at random, here
In March of 1916 shots, and sounds
From burning wood and horses running hard,
And yells of "Viva Villa" split the night
In two: the then of hush, the blare of now.
A man and wife went to the door and died.

Voices speaking from film tell us they died,
They and eight other people living here.
The speakers, who were children then, are now
Old but childlike still when talking of sounds
Of bullets whizzing past them through the night
And of machine guns, near dawn, firing hard.

On grainy film the ground looks dry and hard
Which the bodies of Villa's men who died
Must have lain on as day replaced the night
And flight attack. In time the people here,
Old voices tell us, dared to hope the sounds
They heard implied that all was well for now.

It was for them but not for all. And now
The facts are such as parents think too hard
For children's ears: implicit in the sounds
Of flight was death, for ninety men had died
On soil not theirs; carted away from here
And burned, the corpses later lit the night.

Then in the following week, day and night,
As jumpy film of the time shows us now,
Troops arrived in thousands undreamed of here
Before, along with cranky biplanes hard
To fly and trucks that sometimes balked and died—
Soldiers' doings, these days, made all the sounds.

The army entered Mexico, where sounds
Of chase and ambush lasted day and night
Up and down Chihuahua and only died
Away when it came back. A woman now,
On film, says men brought pets along the hard
And dusty walk from Mexico to here.

The sounds of coyotes' yips are common now;
When night ceases, the houses hint that hard,
Dark times never died for the people here.

Five Variations on a Lupine Theme
(Remembering Robert Herrick)

1

While with the dawn a coyote goes,
I mark his motion as it flows
Inside the coat he sports as clothes.

Then, in a trace of snow I see
The prints he left with paws so free—
How near and far from them to me.

2

At dawn a coyote trotted by,
With steps that any friendly eye
Would see as endless in supply.

The prints in dust of snow where late
He'd been became to me a bait:
Counting, I paced to twenty-eight.

3

At dawn I saw a coyote go,
And tranced I watched the easy flow
Of steps—it seemed the morning's show.

Shortly, I saw a film of snow
Had kept his prints, all in a row,
Wherein crystals began to glow.

4

With fluid steps the coyote passed,
And near the bush he trotted past
A cottontail crouched down, aghast.

The window frame having no flaws,
I didn't hear, despite the pause
I made, the hush, the whispering paws.

5

No coyote ever strolled at dawn
On Herrick's tidy English lawn
In hope of meeting with a faun.

How strange if such a foreign head
Had grinned as rabbits hopped in dread!
And, Herrick, what would you have said?

Canis Latrans
(Suite of Eight)

I

Your reputation, Coyote, never's been
The best. You're mean and sneaky, and you will
Eat carrion, people say; it seems you sin
By taking lambs or calves for lawful kill.
Yes, when you can you hunt down cottontails
Or calves, but not as if to end the kind,
And true, the hunting style you have entails
Surprise and stealth, which others too can find
It in themselves to practice. When you make
A meal of meat you've found, you show you give
The need to eat the due you must and break
A fast with any food that lets you live.
You work in twos to feed and raise your young,
And haunt or liven nights by giving tongue.

II

A coyote crossed the road with neither haste
Nor break of stride, sudden in morning's glow,
Almost aglow himself, it seemed, as though
The sun brushed his coat with bronze as he paced
Before our widened eyes. Without the waste
Of looks at us he moved with steady flow
Of steps, a rabbit dangling limp below
His jaw, then disappeared, not to be traced.
	Lucky hunter and luckless prey. We feel
For one the loss of sight and sound and breath—

Of running, eating, playing, mating—and thus
In thinking of the other we have to steel
Ourselves to read in him, who made the death,
The signs of being of a kind with us.

III

These days you may, Coyote, happen upon
A wolf—your cousin of similar face
And shape but also of the greater brawn
And grimmer look despite his kindred race.
His size and strength have been his tragic flaw,
Since frightening men has made of him a case
In need of help. I doubt you'll be in awe,
For all that when he sees you he may make
A threat against your life; you'll then withdraw
Without a pause for fighting and the sake
Of coyote honor; though you won't forgive
And bless him, neither will you try to take
Revenge, because to tit for tat you give
No thought, knowing your business is to live.

IV

A tawny, slender coyote moved beside
The ditch, trotting at ease; to keep our pace
The same we slowed, starting a seeming race
Not to pass him but to stay side by side
Across the ditch, looking as if allied
Perhaps—with him, though, heading for a place
He'd chosen, since he wasn't giving chase,
And us observing our unconscious guide.

Then he stopped. For a moment of suspense
Before he vanished from our sight he stared
Directly at us, trying to make sense,
We guessed, of what or who we were, not scared
Really, but curious, thoughtful, and intense,
Wondering perhaps if he should get prepared.

V

Daily before dawn, Lon, who cuts my hair,
Meets coyotes as he walks—a snarl or whine
Or scrape, and then he looks and sees them there,
Behind or to the side, with eyes that shine
In faces close and higher than his knees.
At times, they come so near they cross a line,
And then he fires straight up so as to ease
The nerves of all. What's on their minds? A meal?
Not likely. Maybe they just want to tease
Or in their own odd way want him to feel
They're friendly coyote-style—though that I doubt—
Or they think the gray-lit hour on the reel
Of hours, the dusky hour when Lon's about,
Is theirs, and so they come to check him out.

VI

The sandhill cranes are countless, shining gray
In winter sun, save for legs that're dark
And thin and blend with shrubs and trees that mark
The end of the field. Closer, near the clay
That banks the stream, a coyote seems to pay
The cranes no mind while sniffing in the stark,

Scrawny stubble, his dog-like shape a mark
In reddish blond that makes a cheerful day.
    The cranes and coyote move, apart but all
As one, the cranes with slow long-legged stalk,
The line they're in rippling as they withdraw
If the coyote approaches in his walk,
His head and face averted, eyes on small,
Supposed prey on which to clamp his jaw.

VII

You're more likely to see a coyote dead
Than living. Coyotes much prefer the night
For what they do and may get dazed by bright
And glaring lights coming from straight ahead,
And stand still, fearful and confused, instead
Of jumping to the side and off the right
Of way. It's then they're hit and hurled to light
Just off the road, and with no more to dread.
    A breeze walks through the fur; a stain of red
Is by the grinning mouth. With morning light
A turkey vulture settles near the head,
Which like the body death makes oddly slight,
And many other creatures will have fed
Before the coyote's shrunk to final white.

VIII

The coyote's voice is always high of pitch
But seldom single. Two or more you hear
In yelps and howls and barking sounds quite near
To barks of dogs. The coyotes thus bewitch

The night with voices coming to the ear
From far, the farthest edge of hearing, which
They float to small and faint but always rich
In strength to bring the wild, for fear or cheer.
　　Once, though, a howl from near the window filled
The deep gray dusk of the room, breaking lone
And long, starting low and soon reaching high,
Hanging timeless as the coyote, close by
Outside, standing with paws in dirt and stone,
Voiced his voice to the fading stars, then stilled.
Pro Musica in El Paso del Rio del Norte
Here at this crossing where the north begins
And Mexico and the West make a blend,
You hear at times the song of violins

In chamber music, when the traffic thins
With nightfall. For a while then, journeys end
Here at this crossing where the north begins,

Just as they did at nightfall when no inns
Awaited travelers at the river's bend.
You hear at times the song of violins

Where history speaks of frequent strife and sins
Of men with knife or gun as surest friend
Here at this crossing where the north begins.

The notes and phrases in the whole that wins
Applause fill the hall, and as they ascend
You hear at times the song of violins

Or flute or cello as a rondo spins,
Until at last no tones are left to send.
Here at this crossing where the north begins
You hear at times the song of violins.

For a Season, Hummingbirds

At a season hummingbirds are with us most
Of the time from dawn to dusk. They come to dip
Their beaks in the flowers blooming near the house
And in a feeder by a window; they're here,
No more than half an hour's drive from Mexico,
From March till October, though a year ago
Lone birds came along a day or two apart
Until Thanksgiving was just two days away.
    A black-chinned is always the first to arrive,
A solitary male; others follow him,
And then females start to show up one by one
A week or ten days on. He appears, the first,
As easily as if he hadn't just then
Flown in—with rests, of course—from Michoacan
Across mountain ranges and deserts to stop
Here, a sudden and unmistakable shape
Coming steadily down in a blur of wings
Outside the window where the feeder has hung
For about a week. For the time he won't perch.
He hovers, rather, his wings in constant blur
Beside his body, all two inches of it,
Inclining his head downward to thrust his beak
Into an opening in the feeder's rim;
Occasionally he looks up and around.
    His back is a strongly iridescent green,
His head green also, much darker; and a spot
Of white, quite small, is near each eye, which is dark
To nearly black, and always shining. The black
From beak to base of throat that gives him his name
Is striking because from his breast to his tail
He's white or whitish; in the right slant of light
A vivid collar, a narrow violet band,

13

Appears at the edge of the black. As he feeds,
His diminutive feet curl slightly below
His body. When he's ready to leave, he flies
Backward, as no other bird knows how to do,
Rising slightly, and moments later has gone
Too far for human eyes to keep him in sight.
　　　How is it, we ask ourselves then, that he knew
To come? Maybe he saw the feeder by chance—
But how did he know it held a store of food?
The questions are the more pointed when I think
About the first to arrive five years ago:
The middle of March and the feeder not up,
And at the window the hummingbird appeared,
Coming down steadily in the normal way,
Expectant, obviously, and clearly annoyed
At not finding what he expected. He glared
At us through the pane as he hovered and paused,
And we promptly filled a feeder with his food,
One part sugar to four of water, and hung
It out. A little later on he came back.
That year was our third in the house and the third
Year of our giving food to the hummingbirds,
And before we moved in nobody was here.
　　　From the time of their arrival till July
The black-chinned hummingbirds have the food we give
Almost to themselves. Rarely, a verdin tries
The feeder, sometimes an oriole or a finch,
But only briefly. A broad-tailed hummingbird
Passes through once in a while, his wings atrill
As he flies or hovers, stays a day or two,
And goes on to spend the summer farther north.
On a day in nineteen ninety-five, the Fourth
Of July, a giant among hummingbirds
Advanced toward the feeder in slow, stately flight,

14

The humming from his visibly beating wings
Oddly soft, and settled calmly at the perch
To break a fast. "Magnificent" is the name
Of the species also known as Rivoli's;
However spoken of, he was nearly twice
The size of the black-chinned chattering close by.
They hovered on and stared, all but pointed, but
He seemed to give no mind to their fuss, and fed
At ease. Though from far he'd looked somberly dark,
When he bent his head it showed violet on top,
And seen close up his throat proved a splendid green.
He came to the feeder more than once that day,
Invariably deliberate, always calm,
And also the next morning, but never since.
        In the early part of the summer, at times
We'll hear rhythmic, metallic buzzing outside,
Where we know no machine's being used, and there
In front of a mesquite or creosote bush
Or the desert willow planted near the wall
Oscillates a male black-chinned hummingbird, back
And forth, piston-like, a distance of perhaps
A yard, all the while flying impossibly
Sideways—his back's to the bush or tree, his eyes
Stare directly ahead. If the sound's a slow
And steady pulse fainter at short intervals,
A hummingbird is then zooming up at all
The power his wings provide—a dart of sheer
Exuberance rocketing into the sky—
Until having reached the height he wants, the flight
Seeming vertiginous but wholly controlled,
He doubles back, powers down as recklessly,
As he nears ground makes a broad turn up, and shoots
Once more toward the blue sky, tracing a rough U
Again and again, and—without warning—stops,

Unmoving as the twiglet he's settled on.
Is it a courtship? territorial display?
We don't know, but if I could do as he does
I would, preposterous as the sight would be.
     In July the rufous hummingbirds arrive,
Their coming then meaning that they're going south.
In full color, the male is an orange rust,
Changeable to an extreme in certain light.
One, poised three yards from the feeder in a ray
Of the sun, outshone the sun itself, seemed clad
In mail, so diamond bright he was to the eye.
He launched himself toward the feeder and attacked
A sitting hummingbird with his beak and wings
And drove her off; but she soon came back again
From a little distance. Rufous males will perch,
Often, near a store of food they seem to think
Meant just for them and blaze forth to fight against
Intruding birds—success is commonly brief.
     With the days of August the number of birds
Rises, and they concentrate on taking food
So single mindedly that they put aside
Their quarrels. We'll see as many as six perched
At the feeder and even more in the air
Just above them, waiting; sometimes two will put
Their beaks to one opening. These numbers fall
As August ends and then September, until
In October only a few of the birds,
Black-chinned all, stay or pass through. Finally not
A one comes to the feeder or the last blooms.
We take down the feeder after a few days.
Now we await, for a season, hummingbirds.

The Witness of Lei Hou, Violin

(Schubert Piano Trio in E-Flat Major, January 22nd, 2000;
Ruggero Allifranchini, Violin, Suren Bagratuni, Cello,
Stephen Prutsman, Piano)

Slowly the cellist draws a tone to start
A theme, the pianist's fingers strike a clear
Ascending run, the violinist here
Blends in a high and lyric line, the part
Binding the whole, and now with all the heart
The three possess they offer up a dear
Expense of skill, enthralling to the ear,
That ends the trio with consummate art.
     The violinist just ahead a row
Rises and calls "Bravo," her voice—as slight
As she—adding a single sound to all
The whistles, cheers, applause that crowd the hall,
A sound though lost at once already bright
To me, as now again she calls "Bravo!"

Hawk and Handler
(Desert Museum, April 12th, 2000, 1:00 P.M.)

At the same time the blonde young woman nears
The crowd the hawk alights, his wings spread wide,
On top a high saguaro, looks aside
Above her shining head, then lifts—as cheers
Sound out—in easy, circling flight, and veers
Away on slightly tilted wings to ride
In ever broader rising gyre, untied
From earth so far he nearly disappears.
     Out of the blue he hurtles in a dive,
A mote growing at giddy speed to hawk
In fiercest raptor's stoop, while all the while
His talons reach until he fixes, live,
Upon a glove, upheld and shielding—hawk
At hawkish rest, young woman with a smile.

Even so high the hawk can see the sheen
From off the fair young head, and takes his flight
Yet higher, keeping still the head in sight
With every spiral as he soars between
The earth and sky, while mountains in the scene
He looks at change, becoming only slight
And incidental humps that dot the bright,
Sun smitten land he floats above, serene.
     Far, far below, the hand goes up, the sign,
And at the sign he furls his wings to start
The straight, unerring plunge, his speed the best
He knows, the wind a rising hiss, then whine,
Then shriek—until he flares his wings apart,
Seizes the upheld hand, and comes to rest.

Musicians in the Metro

Under the Arch of Triumph, in the great
Array of halls musicians play the best
They can for cash and so set out a plate
Or cloth to passersby who shuttle, pressed
For time, from train to train. The mute request
Is put by youthful players or, in rare
Event, by someone worn, clearly distressed,
Who's eking out a slow and halting air.

From a guitar a young man plucks a spate
Of notes, and many people pause, possessed
By song until the player slows his rate
And ends. The coins and bills they strew attest
His talent while not far, slumped as if dressed
In chains and wan in the electric glare,
A man, a violin across his chest,
Is eking out a slow and halting air.

The rush hour ends. The young man doesn't wait
But scoops his money in a bag with zest
And goes along the hall with jaunty gait,
A tall young chap whose walk and look suggest
A faith in luck as something to invest.
Shortly his paces bring him to the spare
Old man who as the young one comes abreast
Keeps eking out a slow and halting air.

The youth now drops some coins but adds no jest,
And leaves the violinist on the bare
Cement still seeming lost and far from blessed,
Still eking out a slow and halting air.

Border Grill
(7040 North Mesa, El Paso)

Maria Diaz owns and runs the place,
Consisting of two rows of tables, nine
In all, the glass tops polished to a fine
And lustrous gleam that does instead of lace.
Beyond an open archway is the space
The kitchen occupies; the food's a line
Of tacos, burros, flautas quite benign
In use of chile, which is yet the base.
        Maria takes your order, jotting while
You speak, her face not stern but wholly still
Until she smiles—as when a chance of light
Brings sudden life and wholeness to a site
Of trees and pond and ordinary hill,
And then a sudden pleasure, so the smile.

Ballade for Gull and Cellist
(Nina Maria Lee, Cello)

Riding just off the taffrail and as high
Above, the gull inclines his head to right
And left in nods enabling him to eye
The sea, and never beats his wings to fight
His weight but tilts himself by frequent slight
And subtle shifts, hard to make out, that bear
Him always on, an escort feathered white
In sure, dynamic union with the air.

The cellist sweeps her bow to amplify
The quartet's tone; her eyebrows knitted tight
And, with them, lips suddenly pursed imply
An anxious, sad, or dubious mood, but quite
As suddenly she starts a smile that's bright
And wide, and leans far forward in her chair
And smoothly back again to sit upright
In sure, dynamic union with the air.

Then unexpectedly, she rubs her eye
Within a rest occurring at a height
Of tension in the soaring theme, then by
A sweep of arm joins in the final flight;
The constant gull with startling avian sleight
Brings up a leg and foot, all black and bare,
To scratch his head then tucks them back, aright,
In sure, dynamic union with the air.

The cellist and the gull, alike despite
Their kinds and drawn together here to share
A verse, live in imagination's light
In sure, dynamic union with the air.

Tempera on Canvas

Naked she stands aboard a giant shell
That's reaching land, her face turned slightly right
And down, her hair a bronze gold flow to well
Below her hip; out of her line of sight
A man above the greenish sea blows air
To push her on, his arm about a bare
And clinging girl; and on the dusky shore
A woman gowned in gray makes swiftly for
Her side, a dull red cloak in hands held high
And out and both her feet seeming to soar
Somewhat above the ground as she steps nigh.

Venus born of the foam has come to dwell
On Cyprus—though she'll choose some other site
At times—with Zephyr puffing to propel
Her, Flora once called Chloris holding tight,
While, with the offered cloak held up to wear,
The other helper nears. Such acts as rare
As standing on a shell as on a floor,
Or staying up in air and with no more
Support than air, or seeming to apply
No weight in walking, gods may think a bore,
Too commonplace to catch a godly eye.

But Botticelli makes them parallel
Unearthly beauty: Venus is a white
Of pearl so glowing that it seems to well
Within her skin, her woman's breast a bright
Perfected hemisphere just made to bare
A nipple like a bloom ideally fair,
Her pensive face an oval to adore;
And further, Botticelli's maker's lore

Fixes on her the others' eyes, whereby
Her inward look does not so much ignore
The world as put her farther than the sky.

The wrist and hand, however, that compel
One painted breast to flatten, under slight
And subtly hinted pressure, also tell
Of flesh as flesh that feels—that's warm and quite
Alive—and give the real an equal share
With the ideal. The tress of bronze gold hair,
Bound at her neck and then allowed to pour
Along her back and side like precious ore,
Until it hides the place where mound and thigh
And thigh are joined, comes from an ample store
Of feints and visual puns both deft and sly.

Maybe a woman, pretty, young, whose bell
Tolled long ago, lives on here still despite
The bell. She'd come from town, perhaps, to sell
Her work, long hours at pose in northern light
With now and then a break to take a chair
When Botticelli, painting, grew aware
She'd tired. She'd stand naked behind a door
Kept shut, the master focused on his chore
And some apprentices at work nearby,
And have her thoughts on stillness to the core
While brush brushed canvas, quiet as a sigh.

The work complete and standing propped before
Her, maybe with a tear she saw a score
Of means the painter took to amplify
Her beauty and so make her evermore
The sign of what he wished to glorify.

Naming the Mountains
(Suite of Four)

I

These mountains seem an island with its base
Aflame in springs when in the fall before
Hard rain has drenched the earth, for then the store
Of seeds from poppies, buried and in place
For years, bursts forth in brilliant blooms that grace
The lower slopes with swaths of yellow more
Aglow than gold as rays of sunlight pour,
Late in the day, upon the range's face.
    Florida's said today as men would say
The word who'd come from Spain and seen the scene
Of wondrous poppies on a lucky day
Or may, with other luck, have chanced to glean
An image from the natives' speech some way,
Not seeing then what later could be seen.

II

North of us thirty miles the stony peak
Called Cookes juts up from ridges east and west,
The highest, starkest, most imposing crest
For leagues around. A name that doesn't speak,
Except about a man who's for the rest
Nearly forgotten, long has stayed the test
Of use though void of even slight mystique.
    The rugged slopes below Cookes Peak are where
Four hundred people heading westward came
And left their bones for going near the lair

Of the Apache tribe that made a claim
To all this land and fought for it right there.
And now remains the nearly nameless name.

III

Red Mountain rises west and north, a lone
And bulky mass above the desert floor
That's always reddish in the light before
Midday. Southward, in an unpeopled zone,
The Cedar Mountain Range's earth and stone
Make up in long, uneven line a score
Of humps, a dark and hazy kind of shore
Thrust low against the sky, withdrawn, unknown.
　　Red Mountain, part of daily seeing here,
Comes by its name with obvious ease. Not so
The Cedar Mountain Range, whose name we owe
To someone's insight: that a mountain near
Some others, and all roughly in a row,
Is one with them, and has them in its sphere.

IV

Nearly conical, the mountains stand three
As one, as if they somehow were allied
To make an obvious landmark just this side
Of Mexico. Brush grows but not a tree
To blur the forms, and so the three rise free
Into the sky where clouds are rare to hide
Them, from a single base that's low and wide,
A group seeming to draw the eye to see.
　　The Tres Hermanas, named by Spanish men

Who saw in them—aside from earth and rock—
A theme, still have the name assigned them then,
A name that used today gives some small shock
Of pleasure, for it's from the happy stock
Of words too right to cloy when said again.

Quail and Others

The quail come in the garden every day
And in the spring and summer bring their broods,
Close versions of themselves, to scratch with them
In dry or dampened earth, dislodging seeds;
They splash about in basins we've set out
On concrete pedestals and have a drink.
They're mainly Gambel's quail, and now and then
Some scaled. Some doves come every day as well—
Mourning doves these are; the white-winged are here
Only in warmer months. Throughout the year
The pyrrhuloxia, gray with bright red chest,
Red mask, and massive bill, will perch upright
On yucca stalks or on the stuccoed wall
Built to close the garden, but other birds
Don't come so easily to sight because
They forage, as the crissal thrashers do,
And also towhees and the cactus wrens,
In and under the bushes near the wall—
Creosote, little leaf sumac, and sage—
Or else because they hop and flit about
Too quickly for the human eye to track,
Sparrows, verdins, finches and any small
And lively birds. The hummingbirds are here
For seven months at least, swift moving blurs
Resolving when they flare and stop at blooms
Or at the vial hanging just for them
Into the clearest kind of avian form.
      Roadrunners' visits are irregular;
The bird is almost always by himself,
Without another of his kind to keep
Him company, that is, and he is shunned
By other birds. We've seen him catch a quail,

A young one, try for hummingbirds, and once
Himself get taken by a cat, a flash
Of orange surging from beyond the wall
On which the bird first walked, then stalked, then paused.
    Roadrunners don't drive off the other birds,
And neither does the great horned owl who comes
At times and spends a night or two or more,
Depending, we suppose, on how much food
He finds. We hear his hoot, quite soft but deep
In tone, and in the morning find the bones
Of little squirrels we assume he's made
His meal. We've seen him in the final hour
Of twilight, when the other birds have all
Retired, a burly presence standing big
And still on the antenna mounted by
Our house, and once we saw him fly away,
The beat of wings without a sound, the flight
So swift and straight he surely had a goal.
    Unlike the owl, the prairie falcons do
Affect the other birds on coming near;
They come all through the year in daylight hours—
But seldom, now and then. We've never seen
One close above the garden, only just
Beyond the wall, in flight that's low, no more
Than six to ten feet up, with frequent turns
And pauses when the wings just keep the bird
In place, and in such pause the falcon scans
The ground, and meanwhile all the other birds
Except the hummingbirds remain stock still
Under or in a bush—ceasing all song,
Calls, and chirps—and become as dead. They're right.
In driving, twice I've overtaken such
A falcon flying not in chase of prey
But rather with some place in mind he wished

To reach, the beat of wings unhurried, smooth;
I passed below him once, the second time
I passed with him beside the car and just
A little higher than the roof, and though
I drove at more than fifty miles an hour
I had the time in going by to note
The feathers darkening the wings from near
The pale and spotted breast to halfway toward
The slightly rounded tips, to mark the stripe
In brown below the gleaming eye down to
His neck, to note as well the chunky head,
The yellow cere, and beak that's hooked and gray.
     And also at other times quail and doves
And smaller birds make not the slightest move
Nor any sounds but wait in quiet while
A shadow passes slowly on the ground,
A shadow in the image of a bird,
Black on the sunlit ground, with wings outspread
And still—perhaps a raven, or, in months
Of heat, a turkey vulture; neither'd be
A truly serious threat. The shadow might
Be cast, however, by an eagle, huge
And hungry, soaring high but always with
A will to stoop from there even on prey
That's small, if nothing larger shows below;
In wintertime the shade could be a hawk's,
Rough-legged or ferruginous, adept,
Dedicated hunters of squirrels, mice
And rats, or rabbits of a tender age,
But like the eagle not averse to change
At need or whim; at other times the hawk
Could be a red-tailed or—in quite a rare
Event—a zone-tailed teetering the way
A vulture does on slightly angled wings.

The hawks of winter also glide quite low
Above the brush beyond the wall, the flight
So slow as they investigate the ground
That it's a wonder even wings so broad
And long as theirs can keep them in the air.
These hawks we've seen gliding just so above
The garden, in which nothing moved at all.
      A panic sometimes overcomes the birds
That are, to us, the residents. We hear
A great and sudden whirr as all the birds
Fly off, headlong, helter-skelter and with
No heed to where, for some have crashed against
A window pane and not gone on. The cause
Has been a Cooper's hawk most often, who'll
Sprint of a sudden from behind a tree,
A desert willow placed within the wall
That closes in the garden at the east.
Space is the only safety, lots of space:
He's acrobatic, fast in flight; a bush
Or cactus doesn't keep his talons off—
He reaches in to grab or lands on stiff
And awkward seeming legs to lunge and thrust,
Red eyed, through leaves and twigs and brush until
He gets his prey. The cause of panic once,
A merlin, faster than the Cooper's hawk,
Rocketed from beyond the high east wall
And landed on bare ground that was by then
The middle of a site empty of birds
Save one. He stayed a quarter of an hour
Or more, looking about in obvious calm
As if in admiration of the view,
A blue-gray bird no bigger than the doves
And quail that fled, his face without the marks
In brown that make the prairie falcons look

As fierce as they and merlins really are.
We glanced away and back, and he was gone.
     One winter's day this year we heard the whirr
Of wings through windows tight shut, and perhaps
A crash. Later when I went out I saw
Below a window feathers of a quail
But on the window not a mark. I thought
A panicked quail had struck and yet flown on.
The garden seemed to be not still but hushed
And somehow tense. I raised my head and saw
A hawk high up, perched on a slender twig
Of desert willow, perching there despite
A bulk that made the bird loom large and like
A giant as compared to quail or doves,
A hawk with feathers growing down the legs
To near the feet. The hawk eyed me a while,
And spread great wings and rose and toured above
The garden, the wings startling white and black
And brown, the belly black as well, and then
Went veering off on slowly beating wings.
The next day, the next, and the next again
The hawk returned, the garden every day
More hushed, yet feathers from a quail or dove
Newly strewn there on every single day,
And then one day the hawk did not come back.
The other birds took up their ways again,
Though winter and its hawks will come again.

Pot by Angie Yazzie

All of the form is curves, although the base
And mouth are flat. The walls in rising flare
Until they turn to round the widest space
And then rise on but inward now to where
They turn the final turn and so declare
The little column of the neck, the sole
Curve left to fix with all the potter's flair
A form that takes the eye and makes all whole.

A copper hue livens the rounded face,
Hinted red and yellow making a fair,
Burnished surface that sparkles with the grace
Of points of light. And the walls also bear
Dark smudges—fire clouds, they're called—here and there
That match the inner color, sparkling coal,
Serve as accents, but in no way impair
The form that takes the eye and makes all whole.

Micaceous clay, in Taos a commonplace,
Along with other matter has a share
In Angie's pot; one share leaves not a trace
Except the pot: her mind and fingers pair
To coil the dampened clay into a dare
Against a fall, building the fragile bowl
By single patient coils, and thus prepare
A form to take the eye, to make all whole.

After the test of fire the pot stands spare
And finished, symmetry without the toll
Perfection takes, a simple thing yet rare,
A form that takes the eye and makes all whole.

In the Name

Before the many-windowed, gray facade,
The object is a man who's out of place
And falling, falling in the name of God.

The watching lens might be seeing a clod
In what it shows as going on in space
Before the many-windowed, gray facade;

A voice, though, in what seems a vocal nod
Says he's "dark haired," the man in air's embrace
And falling, falling in the name of God.

His shirt is white, his trousers dark, he's shod
No doubt in black as he goes down apace
Before the many-windowed, gray facade;

His body seems at rest—in nothing odd,
As if reclining there with upturned face
And falling, falling in the name of God.

Far down there is unyielding man-made sod.

The man is at an ever mounting pace
Before the many-windowed, gray facade
And falling, falling in the name of God.

Far and Near

The sounds are faint, drawn out, a kind of call
Repeated often at a constant pitch
And coming from so high and far that all
Our looking up to see the source, at which
We guess with hope and guess combined, may not
Succeed. Most likely when it does the pitch
Of wings changed in the sun and so begot
A flash, and even from so far away,
A mile or more, we know what birds we've got
In sight, for to see and hear such a way
Can mean only one kind of bird, the crane.
     They're sandhill cranes, and of a winter day
Only is when we see them. They remain
Here, near Mexico—where it's mostly fine
During the winter days—far from a plain
Well north, their breeding ground when air's benign
And flowers flower. If a flock we hear
Making the calls is flying on a line
That's near the mountains east of here a mere
Five miles away, it can be hard to see;
But if, as happens, the cranes choose to veer
Westward, then they may be seen in a vee
Up there, their flight as straight as if on rails
And yet for all the straightness wholly free.
Such flocks, though, mainly fly so high details
Elude our upturned eyes; their pace is fleet,
And soon they go so far our eyesight fails.
     To see cranes close we go to where they meet
For winter at a place where they can count
On food, a refuge with a marshy sheet
Of water on which birds are paramount
As forms of life on earth, the Bosque del

Apache. There their numbers daily mount
To thousands; those of snowgeese do as well—
Great blue herons, ducks, and eagles come too,
And blackbirds, hawks, and sparrows—all to dwell
In safety, more or less, although it's true
That some in seeking food turn into food.
     At morning many cranes, with great ado
Of calls and—it seems—taken by the mood
To fly, go off and hunt for food in fields
That stretch for miles south and also include
The trough made by the Rio Grande, which shields
A strip of land from drought and makes plants grow.
     A while before the fading sunlight yields
To dusk the flocks start to come back—a flow,
Almost, of birds until the final cloak
Of night—all flying as cranes do, with slow,
Profound, powerful, graceful downward stroke
Of wing and then a sudden upward leap,
The neck so straight ahead as to evoke
A lance, long legs as straight behind. They sweep
At speed over the rising, broken ground
West of the Bosque, make at last a steep
U-turn that heads them south for where they're bound,
And start a final, long approach designed
To bring them slanting down so that they'll ground
Close by the cranes that chose to stay behind
That day, the bugling calls from high replied
To from below in cheerful bugling kind.
As they come close they make the end a glide,
Always wholly controlled, never a drift,
With wings flared up a bit and spread out wide
To slow the going down, which yet seems swift
To us who haven't learned the knack of flight
And see the use of such a wondrous gift;

And last, in readying themselves to light,
They lower slender legs toward marshy land,
Although they're still in coming down some height
Above it; then, they drop, and as they land
They very often have to hop along
For several steps before they stop and stand.

We listen to their kind of evensong
And watch the landing from a platform made
Of wood (at times in cold that has us long
For shelter in a room with firewood laid
And ready for a match), and now they're where
We see them clearly and without the aid
Of glasses. While they glided through the air,
Sight of them as they passed revealed a few
Black feathers at the tip of wings aflare
For landing, and in seeing them anew
We note their legs are black, as is the bill;
The crown is red, and there's some white in view
On head and chin, and for the rest no frill
Of color brighter than a lustrous gray.

The posture cranes assume when they stand still
Is most upright, and standing thus they may
Come even with the level of the chest
Of many men. Much of the time they stay
As still as herons do, but look at rest
Instead of frozen; when they walk they take
A slow and regal step; they seem not pressed
For time, stepping so gently as to make
Their walking like their flight in grace, and speed
They'll do without til dawn, when they'll awake.

Sometimes a crane, moved by an inner need,
Perhaps, or else a wish that comes by chance,
Will spring straight up and high, the sudden deed
Resulting in no obvious look askance

From other cranes and helped by wings half spread
At first and then stretched out to full expanse
To slow the drop the crane will use to tread
The ground just once in springing high once more,
Springing up again and again, with head
Held high at times and sometimes to the fore.
Others may join, and with no sign of strife
They all go on. Since months will pass before
They mate, perhaps they jump for joy of life.

Piccadilly Circus
(1966)

At Piccadilly on that night the crowd—
Good-humored, noisy, quite intent on fun—
Was such that moving through was very slow,
Though move we did, taking our time, until
I looked aside and just then felt a bump
Quite strong enough to've set me back a step
Or two if not for pressure from the crowd.
I turned and almost put my face against
A chest—I lack four inches of six feet.
Above the chest, the face was one displayed
Daily on postered walls, in magazines,
In all the papers of the land except,
Perhaps, the *Times*, on television too,
The well known boxer's face, the fighter famed
For speed and grace and skill and strength and wins
And also for a brash, abrasive tongue
And quips and jibes he often put to rhyme.
        Over my head, and looking off at some
Companion near, he smiled, aglow with cheer
And health, with youth, with certainty so sure
The very air about him seemed to gleam
And sparkle as he radiated life—
In Piccadilly all those years ago.

At Carrow's Restaurant, El Paso

Her sudden laugh carries with ease throughout
The crowded dining room a rich and clear
Soprano tone that lingers in the ear,
Musical, single, and sustained without
The faintest hint of muffling forced by doubt,
The sound exuberant with youthful cheer,
Though from a woman's throat, telling of sheer
Enjoyment and the will to let it out.
    She holds a plate or two, or a carafe,
And walks about her work, head high, with slight
And graceful sway of hips, her steps all light,
And smiles in bringing food on your behalf,
And calls you "Dear" or "Hon," her eyes quite bright
And wide, and seems just ready for a laugh.

Remembering Juan

We see him on the tennis court again,
So much at ease he seldom had the need
To rush for where the ball, flying at speed,
Would go, just seemed already there, and when
He'd swing, with either fore- or backhand, then
You saw a measured stroke that wouldn't cede
To haste but turned a simple act to deed—
His signature, the racquet as his pen.
    He liked to win of course, and always prized
A well-struck shot that gained a point he seized,
But if with skill and luck you hit or eased
The ball past him, his smile—all undisguised
And all aglow—made clear he was as pleased
As you at your good play, and less surprised.

Mesquite

Mesquite in winter looks more dead than dead:
Randomly angled trunks and branches gray
And stark, the scrubby tree without a sign
Of leaves or future growth and sure to stay
That way for many weeks of spring ahead.

In May, leaves of delicate green align
Mesquite with other trees—sudden and spread
Over the whole like lace in an array
On jagged limbs turned fuzzy blurs instead,
Each leaf made up of leaflets on a spine.

Then soon, tiny blossoms come on display;
Greenish, they grow so densely they combine
To form many a single flowerhead,
Each a brush cylindrical in design,
Each turning golden in about a day.

All those accents of color are soon shed:
Mesquite resumes the hue the leaves assign,
The brushes giving way to beans that may
At last be inches long, though rather fine
Than wide, and glisten green from stem to head.

After just a week's or ten days' delay
The beans turn tan with speckles or a thread
Of rusty red, and with summer's benign
And steady heat they turn entirely red,
A deep and vibrant red that's almost gay.

Shortly the beans fall off, the trees define
Themselves by green again, and any play
Of daylight now before the fall is sped
Will show them wholly green. With winter's sway
The leaves fall off, in every year's decline,

And then for months and into spring ahead,
Stiff and devoid of leaves, the tree will stay
With no apparent hope or any sign
Of future, crooked branches all in gray—
Mesquite seeming once more more dead than dead.

Calvary, in Oil on Canvas

Veronese's painted a well-known scene:
High up against a heavy, cloudy sky
Wooden crosses standing three in a row,
Bodies hanging on them, with Jesus one,
And men and women on the ground nearby;
And yet what takes the eye at first is just
Above the bottom frame and center right,
A woman clothed in yellow cloak and hood,
An enigmatic figure standing tall,
So amply covered by the brilliant cloak
Only her nose and mouth and chin, right hand,
And last an oddly six-toed foot appear
Beyond the drape of cloth on all the rest.
    The yellow cloak droops down in seeming folds
That cast slight shadows, and in hanging hints
At what would be beneath if bone and flesh
Were there in fact, the down-turned head and neck,
The shoulders and the back, the arm that puts
A hand up near the chin, the left leg thrust
A little forward—all illusion done
In paint put on by Veronese's brush
Driven and guided by the will to paint.
    Illusion's also in the crucified
Bodies, nearly naked, that hang above.
The posture of one, youngest of the three
And hanging limp and with his head sunk down
And to the side, suggests a corpse. Far left
And near the frame the other punished thief—
A man with burly chest and shaggy head—
Appears to struggle still, legs bent and tense
In pushing outward from the wood behind
His back. Jesus, who's shown between the two,

His left foot resting on a wooden block
Nailed to the upright post the cross he's on
Is partly made of, and his right foot placed
Upon the left, seems not to strain against
The downward pull his weight if real would cause,
And yet his body doesn't show the hints
Of limpness painted in the younger man's.
    The sign above the head of Jesus, black
Letters on something square and pale, can not
Be read because the distance is too great,
Or so it seems; rungs in the ladder propped
In place behind the cross and near the sign
Cast shadows painted on the ladder's side.
    Far left and just emergent from the frame
A man astride a horse seems to look down
At Mary, fainting farther right, his hand
Shown resting on the horse's neck; the horse
As well looks down, with placid equine face.
And next a man whose rolled up sleeve reveals
A brawny arm leans forward all intent,
It seems, upon a woman, young and fair,
Hands raised in grief, kneeling below the cross
Jesus is on, her youth apparent in
The curve of profiled cheek and in the free
And easy flow of movement that's implied
By her uplifted hands. Beyond the two
Young people is an older man, his back
To all, who's shown from knees to head and must
Be understood to stand on lower ground;
He gazes right and toward a city on
A hill lit from above and rising near
The frame. Tending to Mary in her swoon
Another young and kneeling woman has
Her back almost against the grieving girl's,

The bloom her cheek reveals contrasting to
The gaunt and sallow look of Mary's face.
Behind Mary crouches a second young,
Muscular man whose hands are occupied
With keeping her from sinking to the ground,
Although his head is turned away from her
And toward the woman in the yellow cloak.
Partly showing between him and the cloak,
But farther off, a man braces a pole
Against the cross upon which hangs the thief
Who's died, and turns his face up toward the corpse.
The figure in the yellow cloak looks down
At Mary with what seems to be concern,
Implied by hands close to her throat and by
The waiting stillness of her attitude.
        On canvas stretched and sized and with the ground
All stable, Veronese may have worked
From readied sketches, or he may have sketched
In lines, lightly, to put the items of
His picture in their place, the landscape and
The overwhelming sky, the crosses with
Their weights, and lower down people alive
And going on with changed or unchanged lives.
Later began the countless, steady strokes
Of brushes—surely he'd use more than one—
Laying layer after layer of paint
To realize a sky clouded and streaked
With light, the texture and the sheen in light
Of wood and cloth, the density of hair,
The tone of skin in women and in men,
The varied shapes of women and of men,
The import gestures have, with the result
An oil that above all else celebrates
The simple acts of painting, and the craft.

Names on the Mountain

"Cookes Peak" is what the landmark's called today,
And has been since a soldier marked the place
By giving it a name easy to say
In English, though it's true we rarely place
Which Cooke is meant. Quite heedless, we replace
Names from the past, and as we do we claim
As ours alone this wild and desert space,
Thinking we tame it as we sound the name.

Spanish explorers had a Spanish say
About the peak, writing on maps they'd trace,
"Picacho de los Mimbres," to convey
An image of a crag of stony grace
And osiers all in green a commonplace
Of springfed gulches far below—their aim,
To make the peak apparent to their race,
Thinking they'd tame it as they'd write the name.

"Standing Mountain"—such was Apaches' way
Of speaking of the peak. The words embrace
The loneness of a mountain well away
From others of such height, which could displace
The eye, and kinship men who lived by chase
For food or spoils might hope to have a claim
To, since they'd judge the peak a sort of base,
Thinking they'd tame it as they'd sound the name.

The people of the Mimbres, who'd encase
Skulls of their dead in pots that now have fame,
They too would name the peak they'd daily face,
Thinking, "We tame it as we sound the name."

Readings

"The desert is a book," as said a friend,
His words an echo of his father's words
From which he'd learned many years past, but we
Who read the printed word haven't prepared
To read the desert's page—we've just begun,
And get not much beyond the abc's.
        The dusty roads we walk retain the marks
We make, and now we're pretty sure to know
Which patterns in the dust are ours and which
Are left by others' shoes, also the way
Each of us steps, her feet straight on and mine
A little splayed. A road that cuts from east
To west—through sagebrush, saltbush, Mormon tea,
Mesquite, and scrubby grasses growing here—
Revealed the footprints once of several men
Crossing from south to north, leaving the brush
And going into it again, the tracks
Reminding us the line with Mexico
Is twenty-five miles off, although of course
They didn't say the people'd come from there.
        A fall of rain at night, if just enough
To dampen dust, will make the later tracks
Distinct, and some we recognize. A snake
Has made that smooth and narrow trough that curves
To left and right in serpentine; and quite
As easy to interpret are the marks
A lizard's travel leaves, small prints five-toed
And, just between, the line the dragging tail
Has traced. An expert might identify
The snake and lizard both, at least in bluff.
        Land-dwelling birds may make prints too, the most
Abundant those of quail: three lines that join,

Two opening an angle and the third,
In the middle and longest, pointing straight
Ahead, the whole about the length one's thumb
Is, tip to knuckle; on the very best
Of surfaces, a fraction of an inch
Behind the little print appears a dot.
     Cottontails and jackrabbits make the tracks
We see the most, the lozenge shape the same,
With those of rear paws longer than the front,
Set wider apart, often parallel
Or nearly so, and only length of stride
Will tell which kind of rabbit left the tracks—
As much as twenty feet jackrabbits leap
In flight to stay alive. The line of tracks
Is straight, but now and then there'll be a broad
And blurry smudge, strong evidence of fright
Or worse. Looking about sometimes suggests
A coyote or a dog as cause, but hawks
And eagles live here too, not hunters prone
To leaving prints of talons on a road.
     Though coyotes and dogs make tracks hard to tell
Apart unless they're in the very best
Of ground, we can assume that those we find
Most commonly are not the tracks of dogs.
Wandering dogs we seldom see, but though
Coyotes we rarely see at all, and then
Briefly and never more than one, at night
We often hear their barks and yips and howls,
And know they're always here and on the prowl.
     Some months ago we found a line across
Our land, narrow yet wide enough and deep
Enough to show in earth and gravel too,
And absolutely straight. We wondered what
Could make it. Then another friend, who shoots

A bow in hunting, taught us how to read
The mark. In earth just soft enough to take
Impressions well and firm enough to keep
Them, tracks that had to be a coyote's showed—
They had to be because the print the hind
Foot makes is his alone: the pad behind
The toes and claws puts down a mark that has
The shape of a pagoda's roof, with eaves
Tilted just slightly up. The tracks were on
Both sides of the mysterious line that we
Had concentrated on, the line a trap
Had made, the trap clamped in the coyote's tail.

Resident Flyers

Among the birds that stay here all the year,
Only twenty-five miles from Mexico,
Ravens are those you see the most, for they're
Aloft much of the time. A big black bird
In movement in the sky as ravens are—
At work on raven's work from early morn
To coming night—attracts and holds the eye.
　　We also see them perched on top of poles
That carry telephone and power lines,
Or in the clump of cottonwoods that we
Go near on walks, quite rarely in mesquites,
And as high drama on a yucca stalk,
A tall and whitish stalk that looks to be
Too slight for such a bird. A raven on
A pole that's right beside the road may fly
Away, at leisure, when we pass, but if
The pole's a little farther off, the bird
Will stay and may well croak as we walk by.
The sound seems very like a jeer to us,
But ravens, we note, often croak as if
They're talking to themselves as part of flight.
　　When something's there to eat—a rabbit, say,
Dead along the roadside—ravens may bunch
Together on the ground and jostle one
Another as they press to use their beaks.
They won't have come, however, in a flock.
They fly mainly apart but not alone.
See one that's going by, and now you see
Some others, maybe three or four or six,
But seldom more, and all without a sign,
No obvious sign at least, of acting as
A conscious group. At times, though, and perhaps

In courtship, two will fly quite close beside
Each other, wingtips maybe brushing one
On one at times, and swoop and dive and soar
In rising gyre until they're out of sight.
     In soaring flight the raven equals hawks,
Eagles, and vultures, soaring wings flat out
As eagles do, instead of wings atilt,
The vulture's way. The soaring's steady, too.
The raven's ordinary flight does not,
However, have the look of ease a hawk's
Does, or a crane's; it also lacks the hint
Of power in reserve. The narrow wings
Move somewhat loosely, with a sort of flap
That seems excessive for the speed attained,
Yet while you're judging that the bird is slow
The loosely beating wings will take it far.
     Though ravens sometimes fly short hops—from this
Pole to the next—mainly they head for some
Far place with constant, plodding beat of wings.
     There are exceptions to their dogged ways.
Acrobatic soaring in pairs is one.
Another takes a day of wind. Two miles
Away a row of cypress stands, and there
Above the trees a raven, wings spread wide
And motionless, will hang upon the wind,
Rising or dropping a bit now and then,
Just a few feet, for once without a goal
Somewhere ahead. We've often stopped to watch
A raven play the wind so—playing all
At ease, going nowhere but riding high—
And never yet have seen the raven tire.

Silk Purse

Hung up on racks, quite often in dim light,
A thrift shop's clothes are not so much displayed
As jammed away. They're where they are as laid
Aside as death decides, or getting light
At last, or thick, or as too worn to trade,
Or simply as no longer seeming right.
  Among the shoppers there, some may have aid
Of eyes that see a style and line despite
A thrift shop's tendency to put a blight
On thought, and then perhaps they can invade
A city street, a party in a glade,
A concert—all in their mind, in whose sight
The discard's now a costume for delight,
To wear with pride and flair, as on parade.

The World of San Antonio

Forty miles or so to the north and west
Of Trinity Site—whence one day the tides
Of change rose up and haven't sunk to rest—

In San Antonio's world the world divides
In two unequal, somewhat fluid parts.
The Owl Café and Manny's, only strides

Apart across a road, are counterparts
Furnishing food and drink; and people make
A choice of one and tend to set their hearts

Upon it, though on Sundays some forsake
The choice they've made, for Manny's door stays shut.
The Owl Café does more by far to take

The eye. The entry's coin fed games abut
The inner wall, attracting patrons' change
With lights, a hint of gain in fun, a glut

Of color. Past the inner door the change
Is great because the room is rather dim.
Yet even so people's glances can range

On pictures hanging more or less at whim
With calendars and signs (a few the kind
That would in no way edify the prim)

And, dominating all, the green of signed
And tacked or taped up dollar bills in all
The places they can be: the booths aligned

On one side of the room, on every wall,
The mirror past the counter that's the bar,
And in the farther room. At Manny's, small

And simple, focus on the cooking far
Exceeds concerns about the way things seem.
The buns are fresh. They have no hint of char

From being grilled and have a proper beam.
They're thick with thickness made the greater by
The meat they hold, just cooked as patrons deem

The best, the slice of cheese upon which lie
Wide strips of chile, always green, along
With lettuce and tomato heaped so high

A knife to cut with and a fork as prong
To spear with rather than the normal way
Of eating here may not at all feel wrong.

The rivalry that started on the day
The second restaurant to open manned
Its kitchen hasn't so far waned away

In San Antonio's world, here in a land
That once a man-made dawn turned glaring bright,
Where still The Owl Café and Manny's stand

Forty miles or so from Trinity site.

Painted in Blue

The shapes of men painted in blue are on three walls
Two to a wall, bold against the background of pink.
The bodies have straight sides, no legs, an oval head,
And arms that rise straight up and reach the corner made
By wall and roof, a pose to last with paint and wood
Or whim. Within, the pump pumps water up the well.

New Mexico Nine

Among the highways of New Mexico
The one that's numbered nine has in effect
A start in nowhere at its eastern end,
Because it starts from just another road,
Broad but short, one stretching to Mexico,
Some three miles off. El Paso, built in part
Upon the Franklin Mountains' lower slopes,
Is east about ten miles and can be seen
Although no highway leads directly there
From here, but west, ahead along the road,
The signs of human presence are (the road
Apart) the power lines, a building for
The Border Patrol, and its parking lot
On the left and less than a mile away.
　　　Also at left not far beyond the post
A marker reads one hundred forty-six,
Meaning that Highway Nine reaches not quite
One hundred forty-seven miles in length.
Farther for slightly more than fifteen miles
The road continues just as it begins,
Completely straight and crossed now and again
Only by washes, almost always dry,
That make some dips. A very few dirt roads
Come to an end here from the north, where low,
Distant, and isolated mountains rise.
More mountains are south, these in Mexico.
The plants consist mainly of creosote,
An evergreen, and yucca and mesquite,
With saltbush named "four-winged" also mixed in,
But after a rain in spring, if there's lots,
Snake broom and pepper grass flourish and edge
The road with borders brilliant green and white,

Green from the broom and white from tiny blooms
That crest the pepper grass's bushy top.
　　　The long straight stretch ends in a curve, a sharp
Curve northward at a ridge extending from
The East Potrillo Range, a line of low
And rounded mountains north to south; the road
Then slants upward along the ridge about
A mile and curves again, sharply once more
And toward the west, and now continues west,
Mainly, for thirty miles on higher ground
With mountains always in sight, close and far.
On some, on southern slopes, there grow a few
And widely spaced ocotillo, which may
After a rain come into leaf or sprout
Red blossoms at their tops. Coyotes are here
But seldom seen in daylight; ravens go
About their raven's work in groups of four
Or five, or quite alone, sometimes a hawk
Will rise from a mesquite, more seldom yet
A prairie falcon hunts along the strip
Of earth that's clear beside the road, and now
And then an eagle looms above, the wings
Beating in eagle's time or held flat out
To glide. Far up, in summer, vultures soar.
A man leading a horse across the way
South to north would be the rarest event.
　　　Thirty-five miles or so from where the road
Begins, some higher mountains, blocked from view
Before by those close up, come into sight,
A group of three that rises in the west,
And to the north what seems to be a range.
Where the road curves sharply again, and this
Time south, near a mileage marker that reads
One hundred four, it leaves the higher ground,

Going down steeply in a long descent
From which the Tres Hermanas Mountains, shaped
Like cones and single based, show up almost
Due west, while northward stands the island range
That's called Florida. Slightly east and north
A shadow can be seen beyond the range
On clear and cloudless days, like most days here,
The highest point for many miles, Cookes Peak
Its name and fifty miles away at least.

     The downhill stretch ends in a westward curve,
And then as at the start the road is straight,
Now for a little more than thirteen miles.
For a short way cattle appear, a few,
And then about seven or eight miles on
Houses spaced far apart across the view
Come into sight though still some miles ahead—
Columbus, where the Pancho Villa Park
Recalls the day the village got its fame
As Villa's soldiers raided from a town
In Mexico no more than three miles south
Along the first road crossing Highway Nine,
Just yards past mileage marker eighty-eight.

     To see more cars and trucks than thirty come
Along the nearly sixty miles between
Starting point and intersection would seem
A thing to note; seeing fewer would not.

     Between the intersection and the place
At which a post reads zero to announce
The end—or starting point—of Highway Nine,
On Friday, June 13th, 2003,
The count was all of fifteen trucks and cars.

     The yucca were in bloom. Above the mass
Of long and spike like leaves, green with a touch
Of yellow, stalks ten feet or taller rise,

With flowers white and tinged with green that grow
Along the final portion of the stalk.
Thistles growing from two to four feet tall
Were blooming too beside the road, their large
Purple flowers accents against the pale
And dusty green of saltbush and mesquite.
     Along the way to zero, signposts state
Three names, Hermanas first, where once there was
A village and now nothing but a road
That ends here from the north, all dirt. Beyond
Hermanas lies Hachita, half the way
Between Columbus and road's end, made up
Of scattered houses and a crossroad, north
To south. Animas, next and last and less
Than fourteen miles from zero has a big
Hardware store, a high school, and a café,
The Panther Tracks, at which on June 13th
The waitress with a tattooed ankle knew
Her patrons, all but two. Here too a road
Interrupts the highway from north to south.
     Between Columbus and the end of Nine
The view ahead and to the sides consists
Of mountains, hills, and then some more of both,
With here and there the drama of a peak.
The Tres Hermanas at the start are north
A few miles only, while ahead hills called
Carrizalillo stand. Those passed, the sight
To south of west is clear to Hatchet Peak,
A bulky mass heading the Hatchet Range
And very nearly equal to Cookes Peak,
Far north and east. The highway farther on
Goes north a while and toward the southern end
Of low and rounded hills, the Coyote Hills.
After the road turns west again, for good,

The Animas Range stands out, south of west
And near and far, the lowest near, the high
Far off. Before Animas—well before—
The distant Chiricahua Mountains loom
Beyond Animas, well beyond, beyond
The Peloncillo Mountains too, that rise
West of the town, the Chiricahuas dark
And massive, stretching wide across the whole
Horizon and blocking out all beyond.
    A mile this side of them and at a road
Aligned from north to south or south to north,
With not a man or woman near or trace
Of human presence but the roads themselves,
The yellow lines upon them, and some signs,
The highway numbered nine comes to its end.

A Day in the Desert

The air this day is still, completely still.
The desert willow's leaves and blooms droop down
Without the slightest trace of motion; all
The flowers in the garden do, and dust
Come on them in days past stays where it fell.
A lizard enters sunny open ground,
And darts about with no apparent aim,
And scampers off and hides beneath a branch
That broke and dropped to earth some days ago.

I leave the garden by the iron gate,
Which clangs behind me. Then the only sound's
The quiet, married twitter of a pair
Of kingbirds perching on a power line
Close by. The garden wall casts shade, a strip
A jackrabbit lies in. As I come near,
He rises slowly, walks away, his gait
The awkward, humpbacked hobble of his kind
When not in flight, and pauses soon and looks
At me; as I approach he moves again
No faster than before, and goes behind
The back of our garage—and there he's out
Of sight. The only motion now is mine,
The only sound the kingbirds' half heard talk.
This is the desert when it's most itself.

RvR

In portraits of himself Rembrandt van Rijn,
Who very often painted them, looks out
At us almost full face from maybe nine

In ten such works. The face is just about
Round, with broad and fleshy cheeks, and the nose
Is rather thick, though yet the mouth's no doubt

On the small side. It seems that Rembrandt chose
In coming into middle age to wear
A moustache and not to hide several rows

Of wrinkles on his brow, a line that's there
Between his eyes, and eyebrows somewhat thin.
In his fifties he showed himself with hair

Dark brown, and hinted gray would later win
Over the brown. The eyes are large and brown.
    As the face is clearly central within

Every portrait, the eyes that seem to frown
Slightly dominate both picture and face,
A reason, surely, for the great renown

The paintings have. These eyes, as is the case
With any pictured eyes, can never stir,
And yet they look, as painted, from their place

With an intensity that works to spur
Our feelings and to guess at why they're so.
Their darkness and their size, we can infer,

Make part of the effect, but still we know
That's not the whole. The eyes that Rembrandt saw
In mirrors, his eyes, shifted to and fro,

Mirror to canvas so the hand could draw
A brush upon the surface and leave paint,
Then back to mirror, whence they'd not withdraw

At once their gazing, so they could acquaint
The hand with where and how it should apply
A color next, and whether as a faint

And subtle hint, perhaps the sheen an eye
May have, or something bold, requiring light.
The mirrored eyes' intensity tells why

They're so: they stared to make the painting right.

Close

Two posts some half the height of power poles
Are at the entrance of the gravel drive.
On one a hawk is standing, so I drive
More slowly still and stop. Though yet we're poles
Apart, we're close, as close as two such souls
Would likely be, with me the more alive,
Perhaps, to him and charmed he's there so live.
I step off the brake; the car barely rolls.
     And now the hawk without a look my way
Spreads wide his grayish wings and lifts with ease
Into the air: his chest's the hue of clay.
His flight is low above the scrubby trees
And labored—just the faintest of unease—
And in his talons' grip is something gray.

Tethered Aerostat Radar System
(Deming, NM)

When we look up and to the south and west,
We often see a fish-like thing up there,
Glinting in sunlight or else seeming pressed
In black against a cloud, in place in air
And still except for when it starts to bear
Slowly down or slowly to rise up high.
The aerostat is what it is, a rare
Thing, one of twelve, a watcher in the sky.

The border's few miles off. The watcher's quest:
To spot with radar planes that haul a ware
Of drugs for sale, which some will buy with zest,
Others from need. Pilots willing to dare,
Though, take a chance that's really pretty fair—
Often the radar somehow goes awry
And fails, or gales come up and crews forbear
To send aloft this watcher in the sky.

It tells us man is on occasion blessed
With reason: gas found first within the glare
The sun makes, keeps it up; the weight to test
The tether to breaking point might impair
It, should it reach thirteen tons; and a bare
Half pound per yard's the weight of the supply
Of fabric used to spread on struts and ware
And hold as one the watcher in the sky.

The coca grown and sold denotes our flair
For means with which good sense doesn't ally;
Maybe the aerostat is twice a snare,
This one of twelve, a watcher in the sky.

Crossing Sunshine Road

On this morning of early fall I've walked
A quarter mile, and now I see ahead
A man come out from where clumped cottonwoods
Hid his approach along the crossroad there.
He stops and squats, perhaps on seeing me.
   Some half a mile along the road beyond
Him stand the fire house, manned by volunteers
Who may be there or not, and farther on
Some houses, few and with much space between
Them; to the north Cookes Peak juts sharp and high
And forty miles away; the Sunshine School's
Behind me half a mile, while in the south
Rise the Tres Hermanas. No cars or trucks.
Save for the man, all's as it always is.
   "Good morning," I call out when I get near
Enough. He makes an indistinct reply,
Rises as I come close, and takes a step
Or two away from me. "How many miles
To Deming?" he asks, blending in the name
With Spanish. Eight, I say, and he starts off.
He's young, broad-shouldered, with a pleasant face
That shows some strain. *Buena suerte,* good luck,
I say. He stops, looks back, and stares. "I've been
Two days from Mexico," he says and starts
Anew. *Buena suerte,* I say again.
   Now I go south, walking the dusty road
He came from just a while ago. Two days
From Mexico, he said. It's little more
Than twenty miles away. The line that's straight
From here, however, goes across the Tres
Hermanas. Probably, he walked around
Them on their eastern slopes, staying well off

The nearby road that leads from Mexico,
Walking at night through brush as tall as he
In places, dense in places, always with
The risk of stumbling into prickly pear
Or cholla, which is worse—a rattlesnake's
Possible too. And then somehow he came
Upon this road, which starts a mile or so
Ahead, beyond the little rise up there.
  Soon I'll turn back. I walk for exercise,
The desert air, the mountains everywhere
In sight, tracks in the dust, a hawk's harsh scream.

Performance
(Zuill Bailey, cello, Giora Schmid, violin)

The two come on the stage to brisk applause,
Bow, tune briefly, glance at each other, start,
And from the introduction sound the art
The music is with art that also awes
Us all. The runs, the phrasing and turns, cause
A mood and tension gripping to the heart.

All this on artifacts centuries old—
Formed of seasoned wood, for resonance spruce,
Maple for strength—that all the years of use
In play, practice, and in tunings untold
Have put their marks upon, some slight some bold
(A stain or nick), and others, more abstruse,
Which make for special tones that can induce
Belief in wood and strings as somehow souled.

On stage the two play on with all their heart;
Not they alone are present though to cause
Our thrill: the wood that sounds the sound that awes
Has been informed by players past, their art
And hands, whose tones sound out with every start
And so have part in sparking our applause.

Life and Death on the Patio

A sound that seems a crash, both harsh and loud,
Has me go through the kitchen to the door
At back, in which the little window shows
No sign of any harm or outside mark,
But on the patio, six to eight feet off,
There lies a quail completely still, and on
It stands a hawk, its talons gripping fast
The fallen bird. A wind blows hard in gusts,
Ruffling the underfeathers of the hawk,
Which spreads its wings halfway and grips and sways
To stay in place. This bird's a Cooper's hawk—
Small birds its food, and chickens too—and young;
Its yellow eyes will turn to red with age.
The quail's a cock; its flank and breast are plump,
The color of its feathers russet brown
Just where the talons hold and dig, and all
The feathers tiny, looking more like mail
Than feathers, unaffected by the wind.
        After a while the hawk, perhaps now sure
It's safe itself—for it has glared around
In all directions, beak agape and grip
Constant despite the gusty wind—lifts off
The patio with its catch. It labors just
A foot or two above the tiles, then drops
To earth a short way off the patio's edge
And out of sight behind some scrubby brush,
Leaving the patio as it was before—
The wind blowing across the tiles, and gone
The awful beauty of the hawk in life,
The awful beauty of the quail in death.

The View

In Luna County in New Mexico,
Eastward from Sunshine Road you have in sight
The mountains named Florida long ago

By armored men from Spain; the name was right,
They felt, for mountains orange gold along
Their lower slopes from poppies massed in bright

Array—later they learned they might wait long
To see them so again. It's drenching rain
In fall that sometimes brings about such strong

And springtime bloom, startling for this terrain.
Startling also are times when clouds appear
Joined below the peaks in a narrow chain

All shiny white in front of rocks austere
And dark beneath a steely wintry sky,
For then the peaks seem in some other sphere,

With clouds for base and lacking any tie
To earth and to the rugged slopes that rise
Far down, from which of course the peaks reach high.

The mountains, in the hours before the rise
Of light, blot out the stars low in the east;
With day what's been a logical surmise

During the night becomes the real that's pieced
Of two quite different parts, a jagged line
Joining peaks north and south and, much decreased

In height, a long extension north, the spine
Of which is on two levels not quite straight.
In early morning, shades of gray combine

As almost black on slopes that seem in wait
Of light. The light starts burning with the sun,
Which as it rises at its steady rate

Brings to the lowest slopes a glowing dun,
Yellows and tans blended, that rises now
Against the grays—ever so slowly, one

Constant upward flow—but doesn't allow
Detail to show well enough to reveal
The pitch the slopes have overall, and how

They're shaped. The light works rather to conceal
Such aspects of the range until in time
The sun, reaching its height, begins to deal

Its rays down on the west during day's prime
And thus to show the pale brown rocks that make
The mountains' upper third or more a climb

Mainly straight up and long and also break
The surface into folds; below the stone
The rise is steep, and men would surely take

Deep breaths in walking up to reach the zone
Of rock. While afternoons go slowly on
In summer, sometimes clouds that move alone

Across the sky will cast a spot upon
The range's slopes, and always shadows start
Across the surface once the morning's gone,

Moving steady and slow until that part
Of day shortly before the sun will set,
When it lights the whole and shadows depart.

The light brown colors of the mountains get
A little deeper in the afternoon,
But later, when the plain is dark and yet

The sun is up, the setting to be soon,
They turn a gold unearthly and remote,
And then the range appears to have the boon

Of weightlessness, seeming to be afloat
On nothing. Shadows rise then to impose
Their grays upon the slopes—the final note

Of day but one, for now the peaks glow rose.

Out from Memory

Some storks are in the city's zoo, along
With deer and tigers, people too who come
To look at creatures other than themselves;
The storks stay in the zoo but not enclosed,
Standing or moving in the open pens
And also on the paths for public use.
As if to pose they stand stock-still at times,
As tall as boys of eight or nine, the bill
And legs orange red and the head, the neck,
The body white, the wings both white and black.
Their eyes are dark and shining in the white.
They walk with fluid grace in stately time,
Their every step and every motion slow
And calm—perhaps studied, for once one snatched
A cookie from a small boy's hand so fast
The theft was known not by the act itself
But by the cookie's presence in the bill
As in its stately way the bird walked on.
  Over another city's roofs and spires
And straighter than the course the river winds
In flowing through, a single stork flies low
Enough to be distinct against a sky
Gray from early spring and evening's approach,
The head and neck straight out before, the legs
Straight behind the slender body, long wings
In white and black beating a steady beat
And slow, with rhythmic, constant, measured ease;
They seem almost at leisure, yet they move
The stork along its flight at such a speed

No more than moments pass before it's gone,
Leaving an image in the memory's store,
The image joined with others and transposed
To verses now after many a year.

After Nine Years

My chin strap broke, my helmet in his hands
And he stumbling backwards and down—I got
Away somehow, all in a kind of blur
As in a dream, but here I am and free.
　　Some other day I'll face this man whose spear
Pierced my shield, and face his companions too,
All those others who sailed with him across
The sea to here for war because the word
Was given me the fairest woman seen
In all the world, ever, would be for me.
　　The fight goes on there on the plain below,
But I feel faint and shan't go back this day.
　　Many have died and will, and all because
A silly promise once was made. Untrue,
I thought of course. I took her, though, the one
I saw. The fairest in the world? Who's seen
Them all? But she was surely fair, so fair
A god might want her his to dally with,
And these nine years and more have passed and still
She's fair. And willingly she came with me—
I only asked, then hand in hand, the town
Asleep, and to my ship and friends asleep
Around it on the sand. A little time
Only we had before the husband came,
His brother, and their friends. Nine years we've warred.
　　I'll send a servant for her now and she
Will come, as always. For a little while
She'll turn her face away, upbraid me, blame
Herself, say she wishes the spear had pierced
To me, and then we'll have an hour of love.

Once a Rabbit

Behind the truck, some movements on the road
Ahead attract my eye—a cottontail,
I see as I walk on, to no avail
Tugs at a smaller one, clearly to goad
Or drag it to its feet and living mode.
When I come near as all the efforts fail,
The rabbit runs, leaving behind the frail
Small carcass, surely once its living load.

The sparrow's fall is watched, a rabbit's too,
Maybe, and one September day a fall
From high, down past a many-windowed wall,
In Baghdad a boy carried off, the blue
His jeans were at the seat dark from a small
And obvious stain—fall after fall to rue.

In Palomas

You cross a diplomatic line, abstract
Of course, and there the buildings on the right,
Two of them, looking temporary, house
Immigration services, Mexico's,
While on your left a guarded gate allows
Entrance to those who need to drive their cars
Or trucks across the line into the town.
    Just past these bureaucratic sites begins
A street where commerce reigns, a dusty street
Though paved, which after half a mile becomes
A desert road. The buildings on the whole
Are low, some painted violent green or pink,
The older in poor, worse, or no repair,
The newer places rented to or owned
By people who for pay will fix your teeth
Or glasses, or serve a meal strongly spiced.
Some vendors on the sidewalk at the left
Set out serapes, pictures, pots, huge hats.
    People are always present on this street
That's named by date—the day of some event
In revolutionary history—
Though not in crowds. As you come in a man
May hand out flyers telling of the fee,
A special price, that Doctor so and so
Will charge for looking in your eyes, or try
To sell you something carved, maybe, or else
Music on tape or disk. Most days a boy
Will ask to wash the windshield of a car.
Tarahumara women, skirt and blouse
A patchwork of bright red and yellow, green
And blue, sit on the sidewalk barefoot, hands
Stretched out for coins, their children by their side.

The greater part of people on the street
Are men who stand about in jeans much worn,
As are their shirts and boots, not talking much,
Waiting maybe, although for what's unclear;
A few always stand near the bronze you pass
Of Pancho Villa mounted on a horse
At fearsome, awesome gallop, nostrils flared,
Wide-eyed, and mane flying, also in bronze.

Going North

Seconds after you step across the line
The Gadsden Purchase made, at left you find
A parking lot, at right buildings assigned
To searches and inspections that combine
To interrupt the flow of cars that line
The road, their drivers waiting and resigned,
Quite often waiting for a dog's refined,
Black nose to pass their car without a whine.
     Several miles on, the road gets lost to sight
Among some trees. Beyond the trees and west
A bit stand up three mountains with their crest
In cone-like points, while somewhat to the right,
Slightly farther, and thus not quite abreast,
A massive range rises to greater height.

Flagger on Columbus Road

The sign atop the tall white pole reads STOP
In letters starkly white against the red
The panel is. The arm acting as prop

To hold the commanding word overhead
Turns out to be a woman's blue clad arm.
The woman's youthful looking, slim instead

Of thick; her slimness, though, does her no harm—
Her woman's figure's pleasing in this space
Of desert. Nearing, walking with the charm

And grace of youth, she shows when close a face
No longer young; she wears blue jeans, a vest
Of iridescent green over a base

Of flannel shirt, narrow sunglasses pressed
About her temples, and a hardhat white
And straight upon blonde hair that's partly tressed

And ruled; her face is tanned and skin quite tight.
The wait will last only a little while,
She says, her voice soft toned, then answers right

Away when asked, and all without a smile,
That no, she doesn't really like the work
She does but likes the ready, steady style

Of pay that comes to her. She used to work
As flagger, later thought herself too old.
She walks away now, to her journeywork,

Briefly along the line of cars controlled,
Then back again to where she stood before,
Close to the orange-striped cans placed to hold

The traffic off. She sets the sign once more
On the center line and gazes each way
Along the road. Then, with a muffled roar,

A giant eighteen-wheeler, brown and gray
With dirt, comes by the cars; she waves it on,
Some others too that follow on the way.

When these have passed she puts both hands upon
The pole, keeping the stop sign always still,
And looks more often where the trucks have gone,

The lane coming traffic will shortly fill.
Soon she backs away from the center line;
The pilot car appears, swerves left until

It stops; the cars that follow, by design
At modest speed, she beckons on to go
In steady file as they move past her sign,

And helps assure a safe and constant flow.
The cars once gone, she takes again her stand,
Faces her sign about, which makes it SLOW,

And to a farewell wave, she lifts a hand.

Election Day, 2004

The Sunshine School is where we go to vote.
We say our names, and people seated near
The door then check us off with smiles and cheer,
And next one hands us ballots to denote
Our will upon. In booths we then devote
Ourselves to drawing lines that must be clear
To show our will, and at the last we near
And face the ballot box, and place our vote.

This year there's really nothing to decide,
To choose between; that's reason all alone
To say by vote in calm, determined tone,
The war that we began, unjustified
By need or sense, as all the facts have shown,
Dishonors us who live and those who've died.

Cathartes Aura

The vulture, ever in the sky in days
Of summer here, evokes a kind of dread
His looks up close make stronger, for his head,
Bare of feathers and red, tells of his ways
Of eating. If disturbed, he shifts his gaze
To see, then lumbers off from where he's fed,
Struggling with clumsy flaps and lurching tread
To lift a self his efforts barely raise.

Soaring, keeping his wings in a slight upward cant
As is his habit, often tilting to a side
Then with ease to a level glide, he circles wide,
Wondrously slow, in overlapping rounds aslant
The land, using the air's support to pause and ride
At whim in flight that can at every view enchant.

Le Jour le Plus Cour

C'est le solstice hivernal, et je me lasse
De la saison. Le mésquite à peu près noir
Et dépourvu de ses feuilles n'a rien à voir
Avec son vert pâle; du nord viennent les rapaces
Attirés par les petits qui restent sur place,
Rongeurs, oiseaux; le soleil ne fait pas croire
À ses feux—son trajet bas vole leur pouvoir,
Et même au sud un froid mesquin nous embrasse.
  J'attends l'été, jours de chaleur soutenue:
Quand le lièvre va s'allonger sous un buisson,
Quand les feuilles ne savent guère frémir, quand le son
Est le silence, quand le vautour, soutenu
Au ciel par l'air surchauffé, décrit son rond,
C'est l'époque d'un monde à l'haleine retenue.

Un Nom

J'avais dix ans et sept mois quand le hasard
Sous forme d'un Anglais, vieux, juif, petit, et grand
Monsieur, me transporta du vieux continent
Au nouveau. "Marie", dit-il, "c'est l'heure du départ
Pour vous et votre fils. Ici se démarrent
Des jours troublés, fort dangereux." C'était l'an
Trente-huit. "Je vous donne les billets. J'ai l'argent,
Vous savez—acceptez ce don d'un vieillard."

Peut-être nous aurions survécus, mais je pense
Que je dois la vie à cet homme, anonyme
Ici, hélas. Certes, ce n'est pas un abîme,
Ma mémoire—son nom doit être sous une couche dense:
Je n'arrive pas à le poser dans ces rimes,
Après les années le sortir du silence.

The Hush of Art

Columns in Syracuse's Duomo, twelve
Of them, are Doric, meaning they were made
About five hundred years before the time
Of Jesus, and the painted pots on show
In the museum Deming has were formed
By people living near the Mimbres some
Nine hundred years and more before today.
From both the columns and the pots I've longed
To hear the voices sound of those who made
Them, speaking again after silent years.
    Most likely, several men made up a crew
That carved and built the columns; still, just one
Can stand for all the men whose chisels, struck
By mallets gripped in hands much hardened, shaped
The marble—bandy-legged, short, his arms
Thickened with muscle, curly hair all black
Except it's dusted white with powder from
His stony labors, like his chest and face,
His breath quite high from garlic that he eats
With bread and wine at almost every meal,
He sings or whistles as he works the stone,
Takes part the whole day long in talk and jokes,
And every inch the column is, his hands
Have touched. A pot's the work of one, a man
Or woman, either gently shaping clay
In coils, brown fingers pressing each upon
The last and smoothing all the while, both in
And out, while from the coils shaping the pot;
Before the pot is fired the picture's drawn,
A dampened yucca leaf serving for brush.
The potter wears a loincloth, nothing more,
And sits on earth, the earthen floor of what

We call the Gila cave, with others near,
Some also making pots, some tending fires,
Some minding infants brown as they—their day
Passing in easy talk, their voices soft.
  In Syracuse, with no one looking on,
I've stretched my arms about a column, far
As I could stretch, and pressed my ear against
It hoping, though without true hope, to hear
Within that black-haired, dusty man speak up
To tell of what he thought and felt about
His work, about the piece of art in stone
I clasped. Glass cases hold the pots and shards
In Deming. Good, I say, because if I
And others like me handled them, in time
They'd wear to nothing. Nothing sounded from
That marble Doric column. Only stone
Was with me, cool against my cheek. The pot
I'd hold, given the chance, would say no word,
A word which would be Greek to me, of course,
Like those I didn't hear in Syracuse.
    Finished, these lines will speak of me no more
Than pot or column shaped so long ago
Can speak of those who made them with their hands
And skills and thoughts—the maker makes to make
And having made is gone, leaving what's made
With all of him or her in it that went
Into the making gone as well. The piece
Is there, the piece is all. I'll not think more
Of voices out of things, but take a word,
Just one, from English written long ago,
Add with diffidence some of mine, and say,
Go, my verses, into the hush of art.